IMAGES
of America

SCHUYLKILL COUNTY

The cast-iron statue of Henry Clay has been a landmark in Pottsville since it was erected in 1855 in honor of the great statesman from Kentucky after his death on June 29, 1852. Clay advocated a protective tariff in his "American System" on foreign products, including iron. The increased demand for iron in the United States created a market for anthracite coal produced in Schuylkill County. This is a lithograph of the proposed landscaping around the monument. It was never done. When the statue was put on the pillar it was facing east. The committee did not like that position, so the next day it was turned to face north.

IMAGES
of America

SCHUYLKILL COUNTY

Leo L. Ward and Mark T. Major

THE COMMUNITY LIBRARY
PO BOX 219
COBLESKILL, NY 12043-0219
(518) 234-7897

ARCADIA

First published 1996
Copyright © Leo L. Ward and Mark T. Major, 1996

ISBN 0-7524-0231-5

Published by Arcadia Publishing,
an imprint of the Chalford Publishing Corporation
One Washington Center, Dover, New Hampshire 03820
Printed in Great Britain

Library of Congress Cataloging-in-Publication Data applied for

22 74 112 Gift 9/05

Contents

Stephen Girard, a wealthy Philadelphia financier, purchased 67 tracts of valuable coal lands in the Mahanoy Valley of Schuylkill County for $30,000 on April 17, 1830. Girard died before any coal was produced on the land. The trustees of the Girard Estate leased the land to coal operators, but it was not until 1863 that any coal was actually produced on the property.

Introduction

The images in this book have been selected to bring to life the rich and diverse history of Schuylkill County when "Coal was King." Using the images to tell the history of the county, we move from the Girard Estate to Tumbling Run; from the issues and events of the Molly Maguires era to the towns and homes of Schuylkill County; and finally to the disasters that show how a shared history brings people together and unites them in the face of hardship.

The Girard Estate in northern Schuylkill County was originally a series of tracts of land that were part of a land grant given to William Penn by King Charles II in 1681, and the proprietorship remained in the Penn family until 1775. Early land promoters such as Robert Morris and John Nicholson were plagued by financial problems, lack of inhabitants, and the reluctance of investors to participate in the development of their land schemes, and they eventually lost the control and ownership of the large tracts that they had obtained.

One such land venture was purchased by Stephen Girard, a very wealthy Philadelphia businessman, who purchased 67 tracts for $30,000 in 1830. After Girard had completed his purchase, he sent a team of engineers to Schuylkill County to study these lands and to report upon their general character, detailing the number of acres involved, water available, topography, and the mineral content of each individual tract.

Girard died in 1831 and it was not until 1862, thirty-one years later, that any coal was produced on the Girard Estate. The estate leased the lands that it owned and collected royalties on the coal that was produced by the operators of the mines on its property. Between 1863 and 1884 more than 18 million tons of coal were produced on the estate, which collected $5,009,123 in royalties during that period. The images of the mines on the Girard Estate presented herein are an important historical record of the period during which coal mining controlled the economy of Schuylkill County.

The two dams at Tumbling Run were first built as a water supply for the Schuylkill Navigation Company, but later became the playground of eastern Pennsylvania for thirty years until being closed in 1913. With its beautiful setting between Sharp Mountain and Second Mountain, the Tumbling Run resort took one from the wear and tear of city life to the cooling breezes of the mountain woodlands, and was a relaxing haven for thousands of visitors from 1891 to 1912.

Every summer the trolleys brought more than a million amusement seekers to the famed resort, and at the height of its fame Tumbling Run had about sixty-five boathouses ranged in a semi-circle along the northern and eastern beaches of the upper dam. At that time, in addition to the boathouses, a series of major amusement structures consisting of a hotel, a theater, a dance pavilion, a carousel, an amusement hall, a skating rink, and a scenic railway could be found on the grounds.

Since early in the Civil War there had been persistent rumors in Schuylkill County that a shadowy Irish secret society—the Molly Maguires—was responsible for a continuing series of murders of mine bosses in the county. Through the same period, the miners were attempting to form a labor union in spite of a laissez-faire environment and the rampant individualism of the mine operators. Bitter social tensions brought about by differing national backgrounds and religious beliefs complicated both problems. Most of the mine bosses were English or Welsh and Protestant; the miners were predominantly Irish and Roman Catholic. Inevitably, the Catholic hierarchy, from parish priest to bishop, became enmeshed in the Molly Maguire saga.

Franklin B. Gowen, president of the Philadelphia and Reading Railroad Company and the dominant business personality of the era, decided to break the Mollies, and brought in the Pinkerton Detective Agency to do the job. James McParlan, a Pinkerton detective, infiltrated the Mollies and revealed their secrets in the famous Molly Maguire trials of 1876 and 1877 that resulted in the hanging of twenty so-called Molly Maguires.

With the development of anthracite mining, towns such as Ashland, Frackville, Mahanoy City, Minersville, Shenandoah, and Tamaqua sprang up in the coal fields,. With the onset of the Depression in the late 1920s and early 1930s, the mining industry went into decline, and the population of these towns followed suit, so the images shown here are important as documentation of the towns before the economic and social dislocation caused by the Depression.

Many people in Schuylkill County became wealthy as a result of the anthracite mining era and built mansions to display their riches. These people were mine operators, land owners, bankers, lawyers, and merchants. The homes of the rich people who lived in Pottsville were built on Mahantongo Street, while the homes of the miners were built near the mines and leased to the lowly miners who toiled underground.

The images of disasters in Schuylkill County that appear in this book predate evening television news shows, but they evoke the same feelings as the pictures shown on television today. These images are of floods, automobile wrecks, mine accidents, and fires. Some of these disasters are still remembered today; these photographs will bring back a flood of memories to old timers in the county, and will remind younger people just how important it is for neighbors to support each other in times of need.

These images are a small sample of the thousands of photographs in the collections of the Historical Society of Schuylkill County. We hope you enjoy them as much as we did as we selected them for your reading and viewing enjoyment.

Leo L. Ward and Mark T. Major

One
Girard Estate

The Girard mansion in Girardville is shown here in 1875. Lumbering was the principal industry in Girardville until 1862 when the Mine Hill and Schuylkill Railroad completed the Gordon Plane. This early plane provided the transportation that was needed to take coal to the markets in Philadelphia.

The Girard Estate offices were located in Girardville, as seen in this 1891 image. The first lease on the Girard Estate was granted to Colonel J.J. Connor of Ashland in 1862. Connor shipped the first two cars of coal to the mayor of Philadelphia as a gift.

The Gilberton Colliery was opened by Tyson & Kendrick in 1862 and a small breaker was built, as shown in this image. In the spring of 1864 the Gilberton Coal Company was organized, with James Sturgis as the president. Today the operation is owned by the Reading Anthracite Company.

The Bear Run Colliery near Mahanoy Plane, shown in this idealistic drawing, was first opened in 1863 by George F. Wiggan and C.H.R. Treibles. In 1871 a larger breaker with a daily capacity of 450 tons was built. The original slope was 300 feet deep and it reached the Mammoth and Seven-feet Veins.

The Girard Tunnel Colliery was on the east end of the Borough of Girardville. The average daily production of the mine was about 700 tons.

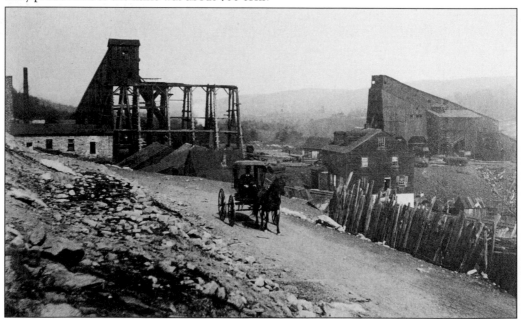

This George M. Bretz image of a horse and buggy being driven through a rocky coal patch gives us an idea of the rigors of daily life in the northern part of Schuylkill County during the 1880s. This would have been a typical scene at that time. Notice the rough fence in the foreground and Broad Mountain in the background.

This Bretz image shows the lengths that this outstanding photographer would go to in order to create an informative and well-composed photograph. Taken at the Logan Colliery, located in Centralia, Columbia County, just a few miles north of Ashland, this picture includes many colliery workers—on the train, beside the shed, on the roof of the breaker, and on the side of the mountain.

Here we have another striking image by photographer Bretz. Although focusing on the breaker in the background, he has captured three men posing in the foreground.

The work of this door boy in Packer No. 5 Colliery is captured forever by Bretz in this image. Doors were opened and closed by attendants, usually boys, in order to keep air from blowing through the mine. Boys of all ages were given jobs around the mines.

The trustees of the Girard Estate made annual visits to Schuylkill County. To take this photograph—in the dark depths of an anthracite coal mine—Bretz used electric lighting.

It was not unusual for Schuylkill County mines to collapse, as shown in this Bretz image. "Robbing the pillars" could have caused this cave-in.

Bretz was the first photographer to use electric lights when making images in a coal mine, but to take this photograph, at the Shenandoah City Colliery, he used the light that was available in the mine.

Bretz obviously had these miners pose for this photograph. Electric lights were necessary to make this image, and the lighting Bretz managed to rig up underground appears to have worked very well. Bretz became famous around the world for the coal mining images he made using electric lighting.

This is another well-composed image taken by Bretz at the Shenandoah City Colliery. This was the first colliery opened in the vicinity of Shenandoah. The first shipment of coal was made in February 1864.

Bretz photographed these three Kohinoor Colliery bosses at Shenandoah in 1884.

The Kohinoor Colliery was located near Shenandoah. It was in this mine in 1884 that Bretz first used electricity underground to create enough light to make his famous images of coal miners at work.

A lift operator at work at the top of a deep shaft mine. His job was to raise and lower coal cars.

A group of anthracite mine employees are posed in front of the offices of the Philadelphia and Reading Coal and Iron Company on Mahantongo Street in this rare image.

A group of employees in front of a building owned by the Philadelphia and Reading Coal and Iron Company. Unfortunately we have not been able to identify the building or any of the men shown here; sometimes such information is simply lost over the years.

A Mahanoy Valley coal breaker photographed by Bretz. Notice the wash hanging on the line in the foreground and the garden in the yard next to the wash.

The Mahanoy City Colliery breaker was built in 1863, and the first coal was shipped in 1864. The colliery was operated by Hill & Harris until 1873, when it was sold to the Philadelphia and Reading Coal and Iron Company. The veins worked were the Primrose and the Mammoth.

The Locust City Colliery, located near Ashland, was operated by Robert Gorrell of Ashland, as seen in this drawing by C.F. Norton of Philadelphia.

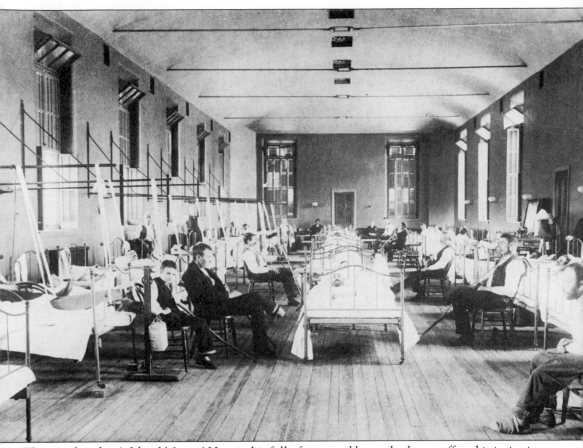

This ward at the Ashland Miners' Hospital is full of men and boys who have suffered injuries in the mines. Notice the young boy on the left who has had his leg amputated.

The Mahanoy Plane, shown in this rare image by Bretz, was the key to unlocking the rich coal veins of the Mahanoy Valley. Coal was hauled up the plane by huge engines and then transported by rail from Frackville at the top of the mountain to the markets in Philadelphia.

This image, a view from the bottom of the Mahanoy Plane to the top where the engine house was located, was made on October 13, 1887. One track was used to pull cars up Broad Mountain, while the other was used to return empties to the valley floor.

Photographs were often taken when dignitaries or businessmen visited the mines. This image was made at Kehley's Run Colliery in Shenandoah on the occasion of a visit by the directors of City Trusts of Philadelphia to the Girard Estate on September 26, 1882. Notice the picks and shovels carried by some of the men.

Many miners were killed in Schuylkill County mines. Kehley's Run Colliery, shown in this image, was no exception. Gas was the cause of a disastrous fire that claimed the lives of three mine bosses. The fire raged in the mine for more than a year before it was finally extinguished.

The Girard Estate trustees are visiting children in Girardville in this 1891 image. Many of the children had lost their fathers in the mines and were considered to be orphans.

The William Penn Colliery, located west of Shenandoah, was opened early in 1864 on land owned by the Girard Estate of Philadelphia. Jacob Shelly, who planned and supervised the erection of the breakers, was appointed superintendent of the colliery in 1865. He was continually in danger of being murdered by the Molly Maguires.

The Indian Ridge Colliery was opened near Shenandoah in 1870 by William Kendrick & Company. James MacParlan, the Pinkerton detective who infiltrated the Molly Maguires, worked in it for a short time.

Coal cars in front of a gangway in a mine on the Mammoth Vein. Two miners are standing off to the side of the cars.

This view of a stripping pit on the Mammoth Vein near Shenandoah shows how large the vein was. Notice the many gangways that had been dug into it.

This unusual 1894 image shows how the trustees of the Girard Estate were taken around to visit the various mines.

This image of the Girard Estate trustees was made by Gilbert Bretz, the son of George M. Bretz. After his father died, Gilbert Bretz carried on the photographic business for a short period of time.

The West Shenandoah Colliery was first opened in 1869, and was then purchased by the Philadelphia and Reading Coal and Iron Company in 1878. It was owned by the P&R C&I Company when this image was made in 1921.

The Philadelphia and Reading Coal and Iron Company owned the Shenandoah City Colliery when this image was made in 1905. The company purchased more than 100,000 acres of Schuylkill County coal lands during the 1870s.

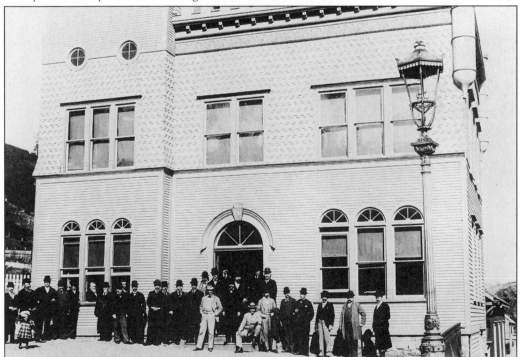

This Gilbert Bretz image of the Girard Estate trustees posing in front of the armory in Girardville was taken on a balmy day in 1896.

This block of coal was displayed at the American Exhibition in London, England. A similar block of coal stood in the lobby of the Necho Allen Hotel in Pottsville for many years.

Two
Tumbling Run

The two dams at Tumbling Run were built by the Schuylkill Navigation Company to supply water for the Schuylkill Canal. For a period of thirty years after the construction of the dams Tumbling Run was a popular resort and recreation area for the residents of Schuylkill County. This image shows the two dams nestled between Second Mountain on the left and Sharp Mountain on the right.

This open-air two-car trolley is crowded with people who are on their way to Tumbling Run for a day of fun. Notice the hitching post on the sidewalk in the foreground.

A trolley stopped at the famous Palo Alto "Y" to pick up more passengers. The "Y" always needed a great deal of attention from the Schuylkill Traction Company due to the heavy volume of traffic that passed through each day. The trolley on the left is traveling from Port Carbon to Pottsville.

Before the trolley reached the "Run," passengers would see the Hotel Mountain View. It was always good for a glass of Schmidt's or Rettig's lager beer. Adolph "Pappy" Naundorf was the proprietor. The building was later enlarged and became the Brokhoff Dairy.

The milkman from the Tumbling Run Milk Dairy used this horse and wagon to make his rounds in Pottsville and nearby towns.

Holiday makers, all decked out in the dress of the "gay nineties," getting off the four-wheeler trolley car at the Tumbling Run boathouse stop. The little boy standing in front of trolley Number 21 on the left looks as if he is ready to head home on the trolley.

The opening of the trolley line in August 1891 marked the beginning of an era of great prosperity for Tumbling Run that reached its peak between 1900 and 1912. During that period more than a million people rode the trolley each season, which officially began on Memorial Day and ended on Labor Day.

The trolley line ended at the Hotel Tumbling Run. Trolleys were not the only mode of transportation at the resort: note the visitors coming out of the hotel to enjoy a ride in the buggies that are waiting for them.

Thousands of people enjoyed eating at the Hotel Tumbling Run, shown here on August 22, 1893. Many of the visitors that came to Tumbling Run from Philadelphia on railroad excursions stayed at the well-appointed hotel.

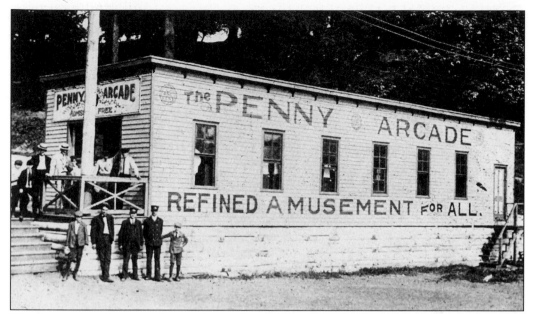

The Penny Arcade was a pleasure house for children. It had all sorts of picture machines in operation and there even were slot machines of the old Western motion picture type. All you had to do to activate the machines was to drop a penny in the slot.

Skating was another popular activity at Tumbling Run. Skating enthusiasts of all ages crowded the rink as the music played.

About 50 yards away from the hotel stood the dance hall, a big building where some of the largest warm weather dances in the state were held. Schuylkill County has always been noted for its good dancers, and many of them started here. A bowling alley was located on the ground floor of the dance hall.

Minstrel shows were popular at the resort, as this June 12, 1911 photograph attests. The Tumbling Run theater also staged vaudeville shows and some of the early motion pictures.

The carousel stood near the landing on the edge of the second dam, as shown in this picture taken on September 11, 1894. Those that rode the carousel often joked about the fact that it never changed a tune, but it was still one of the most popular rides at Tumbling Run.

There were almost a hundred boathouses stretched along the shore of the second dam. These were the seasonal homes of the prominent residents of Pottsville, who would come to Tumbling Run on weekends and during vacations, and the summer quarters of various area social clubs.

Rowing a boat on the cool waters of the large second dam was a popular pastime, as can be seen in this image, which was taken to be printed and sold as a postcard for visitors to send home.

This image of the dam was taken from the dirt road that led to the resort. Notice the rowboat in the foreground and the man sitting in the back—it looks as if he was relaxing while his friend took this picture.

This image was made during the winter when the dams were frozen. Once electricity became available in Schuylkill County, the Schuylkill Traction Company supplied lighting at an outdoor "rink" so that visitors could enjoy ice skating at night.

The steam launch that provided rides on the dam for 5¢ is headed toward the cove in this image. Note the boathouses in the rear.

This image, taken from the road in front of the hotel, shows boathouses crowded along the shore, and the large wooden landing where rowboats would load up their passengers for a delightful ride.

Someone pulled the plug before this image was made! At some places the dam was 80 to 90 feet deep, but when this photograph was taken the stumps of trees resting on the bottom could be seen.

Some Tumbling Run pleasure seekers, all dressed in the style of the "gay nineties," stop for a moment to allow the photographer to take their picture.

Both old and young enjoyed the fun of riding in a rowboat. These boys and girls are posing so the photographer can make what they hope will be a good souvenir of the trip.

The famous "Little Bridge" crossed Silver Creek as the creek emptied into the second dam. The road that crossed the creek continued over Second Mountain on its way to Orwigsburg.

The photographer stood on the breast of the second dam to make this image of the first dam. Notice another photographer with his camera on a tripod standing near the edge of the dam.

This site on the first dam was a favorite spot for fishermen. There is that photographer again, ready to take pictures of the fishermen enjoying their sport.

Ice covers the second dam in this winter scene. Both night skating and hockey were popular at Tumbling Run during the winter months.

An ice house was situated at the breast of the first dam. In 1910 Frank C. Reese, M.A. Young, and H.G. Franklin leased the rights to the ice from the company.

An ice chute was used to move blocks of ice into an ice house for storage.

Ice is being harvested from the dam in this winter scene. Ice from Tumbling Run was used in many Schuylkill County homes before electric refrigerators were invented and for many years the ice man making his deliveries was a familiar sight in Pottsville and the surrounding towns.

There were only a few farms near Tumbling Run where residents lived year-round. This photograph shows two boys and a dog on Tumbling Run Road with a barn in the background.

The Yorkville trolley heads home after a trip to Tumbling Run on September 11, 1894. The sign on the open car proclaims "Baseball Today." The baseball field was located behind the hotel, which can be seen in the background on the right.

A wandering group of gypsies made their camp near Tumbling Run around 1910.

A group of gypsy children are playing in the camp in this image.

The "king" of the gypsies smokes a cigar as he sits on a bale of hay in front of his tent. Notice the stove and firewood in the tent.

Three
Molly Maguires

The Beechwood Colliery at Mount Laffee in New Castle Township was the stage for a number of serious threats aimed at mine foremen and bosses during the late 1860s and early 1870s—the Molly Maguire era. Fueled by labor issues and ethnic animosity, the situation was a tense and extreme one, with "coffin notices" being served threatening death to those who did not "clear out."

Franklin B. Gowen, "The Ruler of the Reading," was born in 1836. Elected district attorney of Schuylkill County during the Civil War, Gowen later represented the Philadelphia and Reading Railroad as an attorney before rising to become president of the company. In 1870 Gowen's company began purchasing coal lands in the anthracite region in an attempt to control the production and transportation of coal.

This was not an easy time, however, and Gowen struggled with organized labor and other forces before turning to the Pinkerton Detective Agency in 1873 in an attempt to break the Mollies. The resulting war against the Molly Maguires ended with the hanging of twenty Irishmen. Gowen mysteriously committed suicide in a Washington, DC, hotel on December 13, 1889.

Born at Mullbrack, County Armagh, Ireland, in 1844, James McParlan came to Schuylkill County in October 1873 under the alias of James McKenna. Within months McKenna gained the confidence of local members of the Ancient Order of Hibernians and was then initiated into the order. In reality working for the Pinkerton Detective Agency, he gathered information which aided Franklin Gowen's efforts to destroy the Molly Maguires in the coal fields and bring to a halt the long period of labor unrest and violence that had plagued the area and jeopardized the coal mining industry for a decade. After testifying at several Molly Maguire trials, McParlan moved to Denver, Colorado, where he died in 1919.

Jack Kehoe's Hibernian House in Girardville is shown here as it appeared during the latter half of the nineteenth century. Kehoe purchased this site in 1873 and the building was a tavern until his arrest by the Coal and Iron Police in May 1876. (The Coal and Iron Police were the private police force of the Philadelphia & Reading Coal & Iron Company.) James McParlan claimed that Molly Maguire meetings were held at the tavern when Kehoe served as the Schuylkill County delegate of the Ancient Order of Hibernians. The Hibernian House is still in operation today as a bar room called the Wayne Hotel, and is run by Kehoe's great-grandson, Joseph Wayne.

John "Jack" Kehoe was born in County Wicklow, Ireland, in July 1837, and came to Schuylkill County during the 1840s. Before moving to Girardville, he was employed as a miner near Middleport, Honeybrook, Mahanoy City, and Shenandoah. A leader in the local Irish community, he was elected Schuylkill County delegate of the AOH. During the Molly Maguire trials Kehoe received fourteen years for conspiracy and later, in January 1877, the death penalty for the 1862 murder of Frank W.J. Langdon. He was hanged in the courtyard of the Schuylkill County Jail on December 18, 1878.

Originally from Cornwall, England, Thomas Sanger worked as a foreman at the Cuyler Colliery in Raven Run. On the morning of September 1, 1875, Sanger and a friend, William Uren, were shot and killed by a group of five men. According to evidence provided by James McParlan and others the five men involved were James O'Donnell, Charles O'Donnell, James McAllister, Michael Doyle, and Thomas Munley. Sanger and Uren are both buried in Girardville.

New To Us

Please do not remove
this flag.

*This item
is not really
new,
it's just
new to us!*

*Thank You
to our
generous
patrons
and donors.*

• • • • • •

The Community Library
Union Street
Cobleskill, NY 12043
518-234-7897

Thomas Munley, born in County Mayo, Ireland, lived in Gilberton in the 1870s. According to testimony provided by detective James McParlan, Munley was involved with four others in the shooting of Thomas Sanger and William Uren. Munley was arrested and tried for this murder in the summer of 1876 and found guilty of first degree murder. He was hanged by the neck until dead on June 21, 1877, in the Schuylkill County Jail courtyard at Pottsville. He is buried in Pottsville.

James Kerrigan grew up near Tuscarora and Tamaqua in the 1840s and 1850s. During the Civil War he served two enlistments including two years with General Philip Sheridan's cavalry. In the 1870s, Kerrigan served as bodymaster of the Tamaqua AOH and on September 3, 1875, he was arrested at Tamaqua for the part he was believed to have played in the John P. Jones murder at Lansford in Carbon County. Although he was implicated as an accomplice in the Jones murder and also in the Benjamin F. Yost murder, Kerrigan earned the name of "Squealer" when he testified against fellow AOH members. After the trials he moved to Richmond, Virginia, and died there in October 1898.

Born in County Donegal, Ireland, as an adult James Roarity moved to Coaldale, where he found employment as a mine laborer. In February 1876 he was arrested and later implicated in the conspiracy to kill officer Benjamin F. Yost of Tamaqua. In July 1876 he was found guilty of the murder along with three others. He was hanged on "The Day of the Rope," June 21, 1877, at Pottsville. Roarity is buried in Allentown.

Alex Campbell came to Schuylkill County from his native Donegal, Ireland, about 1868 and operated a tavern in Tamaqua before moving to the Storm Hill section of Lansford in Carbon County. Campbell served as the bodymaster of the AOH in the Lansford area. He was tried and found guilty of first degree murder in the John P. Jones murder, and soon afterwards was found guilty of the murder of Morgan Powell. He was hanged at the Carbon County Jail in Mauch Chunk on June 21, 1877. His legendary hand print on the wall can still be viewed today at the Carbon County Jail.

ALLAN PINKERTON,
PRINCIPAL.
Geo. H. Bangs, Gen'l Supt.
Robert A. Pinkerton, Supt. 66 Exchange Place
NEW YORK.
R. J. Linden, Supt. 45 South Third Street,
PHILADELPHIA
F. Warner, Supt. 191 & 193 Fifth Avenue
CHICAGO.
W. A. Pinkerton,
Clarence A. Seward, Attorney and Counsel for the Agency,
29 Nassau St. New York

PINKERTON'S NATIONAL

We never sleep.

DETECTIVE AGENCY.

LIST OF FUGITIVE MOLLIE MAGUIRES,
1879.

WILLIAM LOVE.—Murderer of Thos. Gwyther, at Girardville, Pa., August 14th, 1875. Is a miner and boatman; 26 years old; 5 ft. 9 in. high; medium build; weighs about 150 lbs.; light complexion; grey eyes; yellow hair; light mustache; has a scar from burn on left side of neck under chin, and coal marks on hands; thin and sharp features; generally dresses well. Lived at Girardville, Schuylkill Co., Pa.

THOMAS HURLEY.—Murderer of Gomer Jamas, August 14th, 1875. Is a miner; 25 years old; 5 ft. 8 in. high; well built; weighs about 160 lbs.; sandy complexion and hair; small piercing eyes; smooth face; sharp features; large hands and feet; wears black hat and dark clothes; lived at Shenandoah, Schuylkill Co., Pa.

MICHAEL DOYLE.—Murderer of Thomas Sanger and Wm. Uren, September 1st, 1875. Is a miner; 25 years old; 5 ft. 5 in. high; medium built; dark complexion; black hair and eyes; full round face and head; smooth face and boyish looking generally; wears a cap. Lived at Shenandoah.

JAMES, ALIAS FRIDAY O'DONNELL.—Murderer of Sanger and Uren, is 26 years old; 5 ft. 10½ in. high; slim built; fair complexion; smooth face; dark eyes; brown hair; generally wears a cap; dresses well; is a miner and lived at Wiggan's Patch, Pa.

JAMES McALLISTER.—Murderer of Sanger and Uren, is 27 years old; 5 ft. 8 in. high; stout built; florid complexion; full broad face, somewhat freckled; light hair and moustache; wears a cap and dark clothes, lived at Wiggan's Patch, Pa.

JOHN, ALIAS HUMPTY FLYNN.—Murderer of Thomas Devine, October 11th, 1875, and Geo. K. Smith, at Audenreid, November 5th, 1863. Is 53 years old; 5 ft. 7 or 8 in high; heavy built; sandy hair and complexion; smooth face; large nose; round shouldered and almost humpbacked. Is a miner and lived at New Philadelphia, Schuylkill Co., Pa.

JERRY KANE.—Charged with conspiracy to murder. Is 38 years old; 5 ft. 7 in. high; dark complexion; short brown hair; sharp features; sunken eyes; roman nose; coal marks on face and hands; wears black slouch hat; has coarse gruff voice. Is a miner and lived at Mount Laffee, Pa.

FRANK KEENAN.—Charged with conspiracy to murder. Is 31 years old; 5 ft. 7 in. high; dark complexion; black hair, inclined to curl and parted in the middle; sharp features; slender but compactly built; wears a cap and dark clothes. Is a miner and lived at Forrestville, Pa.

WILLIAM GAVIN.—Charged with conspiracy to murder. Is 42 year old; 5 ft. 8 in. high; sandy hair and complexion; stout built; red chin whiskers; face badly pock-marked; has but one eye; large nose; formerly lived at Big Mine Run, Pa. Is a miner. Wears a cap and dark clothes.

JOHN REAGAN.—Murderer of Patrick Burns at Tuscarora, April 15th, 1870. About 5 ft. 10 or 11 in. high; 40 years old; small goatee; stoop shouldered; dark hair, cut short; coal marks on hands and face; has a swinging walk; wears shirt collar open at the neck.

THOMAS O'NEILL.—Murderer of Patrick Burns, at Tuscarora, April 15th, 1870. About 5 ft. 9 in. high; 35 years old; light hair; very florid complexion; red moustache and think red goatee; stoop shouldered; walks with a kind of a jerk; think has some shot marks on back of neck and wounded in right thigh.

PATRICK B. GALLAGHER, ALIAS PUG NOSE PAT.—Murderer of George K. Smith, at Audenreid, November 5th, 1863. About 5 ft. 8 in. high; medium built; dark complexion and hair; latter inclined to curl; turned up nose; thick lips; wears a frown on his countenance; large coal cut across the temple; from 32 to 35 years old; has been shot in the thigh.

Information may be sent to me at either of the above offices,

ALLAN PINKERTON.

In 1879 the Pinkerton Detective Agency issued this list of fugitive Molly Maguires. Robert Linden, the new superintendent of Pinkerton's Philadelphia office, spent several years trying to track these individuals down. Of the men listed here, only Thomas Hurley was actually found. Hurley, who admitted to having committed the murder of Gomer James at Shenandoah, committed suicide in the Gunnison, Colorado, jail in 1886.

Judge Cyrus L. Pershing was born in Westmoreland County, Pennsylvania, and became a prominent lawyer in Cambria County. During the Civil War he served as a Democratic legislator for Pennsylvania. In 1872 Pershing was elected President Judge of Schuylkill County, and in 1875 he lost the race for governor to Republican John F. Hartranft. Pershing presided over the Molly Maguire trials in Schuylkill County. He has been criticized by revisionist historians for his biased feeling for the prosecution of the Molly Maguires.

This photograph dates from the 1880s and shows the Schuylkill County Jail on the left and the courthouse—in which the Molly Maguire trials were held—on the right. The jail is still in use today, but the courthouse was replaced in 1889. Notice a barren Lawton's Hill on the right.

The gallows was erected alongside the east wall of the jail building in the yard of the Schuylkill County Jail at Pottsville. Although the date of this image is not known, it vividly illustrates the horror of the Molly Maguire hangings.

The Penn Hall hotel was located at the northwest corner of Centre Street and Howard Avenue in Pottsville. The hotel welcomed many celebrities as guests during its 130 years of operation. It was the temporary home of James McKenna and his bodyguards (the Coal and Iron Police) during the Molly Maguire trials in 1876.

Young George Gowen Parry, grandson of Judge Edward Owen Parry, gazed out of the window on the third floor of the house on the right at the Penn Hall Hotel, which was directly across Centre Street. Young Parry would watch McKenna taking his daily constitutional on the roof of the hotel with his bodyguards during the Molly Maguire trials. Because of the hysteria of the times, his grandfather warned him not to tell anyone.

In 1994 the Historical Society of Schuylkill County conducted a mock trial of Jack Kehoe. This photograph shows the Coal and Iron Police, portrayed by John Richards (left) and Edward Thomas (right), bringing Jack Kehoe, portrayed by Mark Major, into the courtroom at the beginning of the trial.

A packed courtroom listens closely to a prosecution witness during the Kehoe mock trial. Kehoe was on trial for the murder of Frank W.S. Langdon that took place at Audenreid in 1862.

Attorney Kent Watkins establishing the prosecution's case during the opening arguments of the Kehoe trial. Presiding over the 1994 mock trial was Senator Frederick Hobbs of Pottsville, who is seen in the background of this image. The case was tried using current rules of law with the original trial testimony.

Jack Kehoe (at left) awaits the verdict of the jury as attorney William Reiley looks on. A nine-man jury deliberated for thirty minutes before rendering their verdict. As the "Not Guilty" verdict was announced, the courtroom exploded into noise, with much cheering and clapping of hands.

Four
Schuylkill County Towns

The Mahanoy House in Ashland was built by Judge Rahn on the southwest corner of Centre and Seventh Streets in 1855. It was the second brick building in the town. In the rear of this building stood the old Rodenberger Tavern, and near it ran the stage road between Pottsville and Catawissa.

The men, hotel, and bar room in this image remain unidentified, but they were located in Ashland. In 1857, when the village consisted of about 500 buildings and a population of 3,500, a borough charter was sought.

The store and warehouse of George Mortimer's Hotel Store & Warehouse in Ashland accommodated the needs of the collieries that were located in the town.

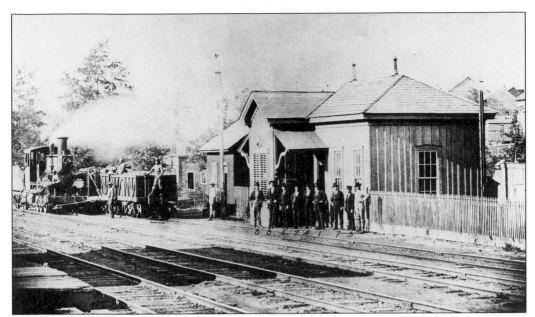

Late nineteenth-century travelers wanting to take a "short cut" between Pottsville and any point north of Broad Mountain would get off the train at the Frackville Railroad Station. From that town they would take a stage that connected with the railways at Mahanoy Plane and Shenandoah. This image dates from 1877.

The construction of the Mine Hill and Schuylkill Haven Railroad and the development of the Gordon Plane made Gordon an important railroad village. The plane was completed in 1855, and was used to transport coal over Broad Mountain.

The McKnights of Reading founded the village of Gordon, naming it in honor of Judge Gordon of Reading.

The plane lifted between 1,500 and 2,000 loaded coal cars over the mountain every day, and it played an important role in the early development of the coal industry in the Mahanoy Valley. This is a Gordon Plane shifter.

Mahanoy City in 1867

This image of Mahanoy City was made in 1867—only eight years after the town was settled. Mahanoy City quickly became the center of the mining district, with five collieries in its vicinity and a population of 6,892 by 1880.

These boys are lined up in front of F.B. Wagner's store in Mahanoy City. The uniforms look great.

This turn-of-the-century photograph of a group of Schuylkill County young ladies was taken near Mahanoy City. The girls are Emma Price (Lost Creek), Janet Mager (Audenreid), Addie Nicholas (Lost Creek), Jessie Price (Lost Creek), Lizzie Homshy (Mahanoy City), Verna Niltanis (Delphi, Indiana), and Emily Buker (Mahanoy City).

"Si" Foster was the coach of the 1922 Mahanoy City High School track team.

The fourth grade class of the Center Street annex is shown here in 1911. All the kids—in those days they were called scholars—are holding their books open. Perhaps they are going to read for the photographer.

A family and two priests gathered around the casket of a miner at a Mahanoy City funeral. The mines claimed many lives over the years, making events like this one a more common sight than was usual for the times.

DELANO COLLIERY, NEAR MAHANOY CITY
J & O. O. BOWMAN.

The Delano Colliery near Mahanoy City, owned and operated by J. & O.O. Bowman, was typical of the many small collieries in the Mahanoy Valley.

The Knights of the Golden Eagle were having a convention in Mahanoy City when this image was made in 1882.

The Knights of the Golden Eagle parade was halted when this image was made, also in 1882. Note that the banner on the left is being carried by the lodge from Allentown.

Those involved with the Washington Hook & Ladder Company No. 1 of Mahanoy City were obviously proud of their new equipment carrier when it was put in service on June 20, 1973. Pictured here are, from left to right: Howell Davis, William Rhoades, Eck, Paul Macleary, and Earl Berger.

Mahanoy City is long and narrow. This photograph, taken on July 15, 1972, shows the view looking down Centre Street from the east end of town.

Heckscherville, located in Cass Township, was laid out by the Forest Improvement Company. It was also the scene of much draft resistance during the Civil War, and troops were brought into the village to enforce the draft.

These homes in Minersville were typical of those that were built by the coal mining companies for the miners, who would lease them from their employers. They were very rudely built, but the miners made additions to them and planted gardens in their yards.

Minersville was founded in 1830 by Titus Bennet. The first settler here was Thomas Reed, who came in March 1793. Reed built a sawmill on the west branch of the Schuylkill River, just below the mouth of Wolf Creek, and a log house nearby.

This photograph shows various aspects of Minersville as it appeared *c.* 1880. The passenger train is on North Street. The three-story building with the turret is the Union Hotel. To the right of the hotel is Dengler's blacksmith shop.

This large crowd jammed the street when Minersville had its Super Sunday on September 13, 1981. Many towns in Schuylkill County hold events such as this where people can come for some entertainment.

West West falls near Llewellyn was a popular place for people to cool themselves in the summertime, as shown in this *c.* 1897 image. Notice the couple sitting on the rocks in the upper right-hand corner.

This drawing appeared in the *Beers Atlas of Schuylkill County*, published in 1875. It shows: (top) Mrs. Jane Grant's Victorian mansion in Shenandoah; (bottom left) Jonathan Wasley, president of the Shenandoah Valley Bank, who was killed in a mine accident; (bottom right) the home of Charles F. Kopitzsch of Pottsville, owner of a soap factory.

The quality of Shenandoah's streets was very poor in the late nineteenth century, as seen in this c. 1891 image of the road that is today known as West Laurel Street. Shenandoah was the center of Molly Maguire activities during the 1860s and 1870s.

Shenandoah was a mining town, as this street scene attests. Notice the trestle for coal cars in the upper right of this image. Life in the town was hard, as evidenced by the bare feet of the children pictured here.

The Shenandoah Phoenix Fire Company was on Jardin Street. This postcard was sent to Joe Lewis in Graterford, Pennsylvania, using just 1¢ for postage.

These Shenandoah folk were in Atlantic City, New Jersey, for a vacation when this image was made by William John of 22 South Arkansas Avenue. It looks like the men are ready for a dip in the ocean.

This view is looking south toward the Centre Street railroad crossing on October 13, 1916. Notice the crossing gates and the watchman's shed on the left of the image. When a train came the watchman had to lower the gates and stop all traffic until the train had passed safely.

The Columbia Hose Company No. 1 of Shenandoah put this new Hahn fire truck into service on January 26, 1974. The company was officially organized at the borough council rooms on August 1, 1870. The borough immediately erected a hose house, which was occupied by the company on November 28, 1870. It then received its first hose carriage in December of that year.

Fire struck Shenandoah on February 4, 1953, as seen in this image. The Columbia Brewery and the church on the left survived the fire. The brewery is no longer in business.

This June 23, 1982 photograph shows a nursing home under construction in Shenandoah.

This doll house was built in Tamaqua and was modeled after a home in the town. It belonged to the little girl who is holding the sign that reads "Aint this nice." The doll house is on display at the Historical Society of Schuylkill County.

The renovations of the Majestic House in Tamaqua were underway when this photograph was taken on November 15, 1980. The renovations included a new top floor, a new sidewalk, and a new front entrance.

It looks like the horses and wagons of this early road-building project near Tremont are being used to take away the side of a hill.

No buildings of any consequence were erected at Tremont until 1844. In 1848 the first post office was established, with John B. Zeigbach as postmaster. The borough was incorporated in 1866. Tremont was surrounded with extensive mining operations during the heyday of anthracite mining.

Five
Homes

This is the Robert Allison home on Pike Street in Port Carbon. Allison, a highly skilled mechanic, owned the Franklin Iron Works in Port Carbon by 1878. His firm made machinery and pumps that were used in Schuylkill County mines. He attained an excellent reputation for the special mining machinery, which he patented and distributed to Australia, New Zealand, South America, and Europe. His Port Carbon business employed one hundred people.

The Martin Dreibelbis house was built in 1780 near the corner of West Main and Charles Streets in Schuylkill Haven. Dreibelbis was one of the first settlers in the town.

One of the first houses built in Pottsville was the Frick home at South Centre and Mauch Chunk Streets. It was erected in 1812 by Benjamin Pott, the son of Pottsville's founder, John Pott. The house was occupied for a time by Colonel Jacob Frick, hence the name by which it is now known by historians. In 1949 Frick's daughter sold it so that it could be torn down to make way for a gas station.

The first public house in New Ringgold was kept by Charles Focht in this small building. It was regarded as a great convenience by the teamsters hauling coal over the Little Schuylkill Railroad by horse power.

One of the landmarks on Mahantongo Street is the Braun School of Music. The Braun School is one of three mansions that were erected about 1847 by John Pinkerton, a coal operator. The homes were known as the Pinkerton cottages. Notice the four Corinthian columns on the front of this stately home.

This image of the Charles Wiltrout residence at the northeast corner of Main and St. John Streets in Schuylkill Haven was made about 1894. The house was torn down in 1904 and the First National Bank was erected on its site. Mr. Wiltrout is the man standing on the right.

A group of children gather in front of an early miner's home near Minersville.

Cloud Home stands on Sharp Mountain in the southern part of Pottsville. It was built about 1830 by John Bannan, a Pottsville lawyer. His wife named it Cloud Home because it is so high on the mountain that it is near the clouds.

Stanley Bright, a wealthy hardware merchant, built this mansion at 520 South Centre Street in Pottsville. The building still stands and is now used as an apartment house.

The home of R.C. Luther stands at 504 Mahantongo Street. Luther was a vice-president of the Philadelphia and Reading Coal and Iron Company, and from his office at 200 Mahantongo Street he could see his impressive home. Today the home is owned by St. Patrick's Church, and it is used to feed poor people.

The Seltzer Packing Company was started by Albert W. Seltzer in 1886. In 1887 Seltzer and his brother erected a plant at Water and Temple Streets in the Jalapa section of Pottsville. As was usual in the Victorian era, Seltzer built a mansion on North Centre Street as testimony to his success. Today Mary Queen of Peace Church stands on this site.

The Dengler mansion stood at 705 Mahantongo Street. Charles Dengler and his wife bought the home for $2,200 from Merdie Work on April 4, 1865. In 1987 the building (then being used as an apartment house) was badly damaged by fire.

The 800 block on the north side of Mahantongo Street is shown here in a photograph taken on October 24, 1989. The style of these buildings is typical of the architecture of many homes in Schuylkill County.

The Reber home can be found farther up the street at 900 Mahantongo Street. Notice the very square architecture of the home, and the iron fence in front of it. There are still many examples of iron fences in Schuylkill County.

This fine example of a stone house is located at 1112 Mahantongo Street. Many of the early homes in Pottsville were built of the native stone that was found here.

These row homes are opposite the Mary Queen of Peace Church on North Centre Street. There are similar row homes across the county.

The D.G. Yuengling and Son Brewery, founded in 1829, is the oldest brewery in the country. Frank Yuengling built this mansion in 1914. He took over the helm of the brewery following the death of his father in 1899 and managed it for sixty-four years until 1963. The Yuengling family later donated the mansion to the Schuylkill County Council for the Arts.

A.C. Milliken was a coal operator who built this Victorian mansion on Greenwood Hill, overlooking Pottsville. During the Spanish influenza epidemic of 1918 the home was used as a hospital, with tents set up on the grounds to treat the children who were ill with the disease.

The Diem home was located at the northwest corner of 15th and Mahantongo Streets. Notice the two-storied back porch on the home. People could sit on the top porch and enjoy a wonderful view of Broad Mountain.

The O'Hara farm was located in the Panther Valley west of Cressona. Dr. O'Hara was the father of John O'Hara, the famous Pottsville novelist. The family lost the farm after the death of Dr. O'Hara.

The house on the Walker estate in East Mount Carbon was modeled after a cottage in England. Notice the chapel in the background. The buildings were torn down in 1951 to make way for the construction of Route 61.

The Mahoney Hotel, seen in the background in this photograph, was located at Darkwater, a short distance north of Saint Clair on the road to Frackville. Miners who worked in the coal mines in New Castle Township and Saint Clair lived in the home on the right. The Reading Railroad tracks can be seen on the left of this scene.

No, this house is not made out of ivy, but it looks as though it is! It is the James Paris home at 132 Boston Run in Mahanoy Township.

"Long Shadows," the residence of Mrs. James Curran on Howard Avenue in Pottsville, was photographed on a very snowy winter day.

This bucolic scene looks as if it was painted by an artist. The large building on the left is the Hornickel Hotel at Germantown. The Schnerring vineyards are climbing up the hill in the center of the image as the road goes off into the distance.

The first house in Tamaqua was built by Burkhardt Moser Jr. in 1801. The people on the porch are members of the Tamaqua Historical Society. They have recently purchased the home and plan to open it to visitors.

This photograph of an old miner's home in Mount Pleasant, Foster Township, was taken on December 1, 1987. It was one of a group of homes that were built out of stone, which was very unusual because most homes built for miners were made of roughly cut wood.

The S.S. Carl general store in Spring Glen is shown here on January 6, 1932. Notice the swing on the porch of the house on the right. Swings were very popular at one time.

This mansion, located at the corner of Mahantongo and Eighth Streets, is a familiar landmark. The wealthiest people in the county, who made their money from coal mining, built many houses like this on Mahantongo Street in Pottsville.

This little house sits in the Yuengling Park at Mahantongo and Tenth Streets. The park was the source of the water used in the Yuengling Brewery.

Six

Disasters

The high water levels created by the "flash" flood which inundated the Railroad Street and East Norwegian Street area of Pottsville on June 23, 1888, were exceeded only by floods in 1863 and 1935. The heavy rains washed 150 tons of coal onto Hotel Street, and caused damage that cost more than $50,000 to repair. The man standing in the flood to show how deep it was does not seem concerned about the danger of standing in such high water! Note the Standard Publishing House at 120 East Norwegian Street on the left in the rear of the image.

This photograph of the flood of 1888 shows the Reading Railroad Station on the left and a crowd assembled near Railroad Street looking at the flood waters of the Norwegian Creek running alongside the street.

On July 9, 1935, the Norwegian Creek overran its banks again. This photograph, taken on that fateful day, shows an abandoned truck on Railroad Street with the Reading Railroad Station in the background.

This car was abandoned in front of the Hotel Davis at the corner of East Market and Railroad Streets during the flood of 1935. The hotel was torn down a few years ago, and today the site is used as a parking lot.

It looks as if the Mechanicsville bus was abandoned in front of the Reading Railroad Station on East Norwegian Street. The large building in the background is the old Pottsville Shops. It was torn down in the 1950s and a convenience store now stands on the site at the corner of Route 61 and East Norwegian Street.

The Long Run Creek overflowed at the corner of Columbia and South Berne Streets in Schuylkill Haven on May 20, 1894. The Freed house, seen in the center of the image, was surrounded by the flood waters.

Landingville, a community located south of Schuylkill Haven, suffered when the Schuylkill River flooded in the mid-1940s. The river overflowed frequently during that period. Today there is a dam in the town that is popular with boaters.

A garbage truck rams through a flooded section of Mauch Chunk Street in Pottsville on November 4, 1982, to the obvious dismay of local residents. Cars had water up to their doors and the homes on the south side of the street were very close to being flooded.

The turbulent waters of the Wabash Creek and the Schuylkill River turned Tamaqua's business district into a lake on August 19, 1955. Streets, alleyways, gardens, and fences disappeared in a sea of moving water as the Schuylkill River overflowed its banks in the northern section of the borough.

Broad Street in the heart of Tamaqua during the 1955 flood. It looks like a car has been abandoned in the flood waters near the railroad track. The crossing gates for the railroad were up when this photograph was taken, but they should probably have been down to stop the traffic!

This section of Route 309, crumbled in the swirling waters of the Schuylkill River, looks as if it has been smashed by a gigantic fist. The telephone construction crews are making emergency repairs to restore service to local residents.

The rushing waters of the flood picked up this boxcar, carried it about 500 yards, and tossed it into the smashed bridge near the Tamaqua railroad yards.

On January 18, 1895, there was a mine cave-in at Audenreid. Old mines would cave in quite frequently across Schuylkill County.

The Gilberton mine disaster occurred at this colliery on January 21, 1935, when a gas explosion killed thirteen miners and injured seventy-one. Between 1870 (when officials began keeping records) and 1993 there were 30,095 deaths in Schuylkill County mines.

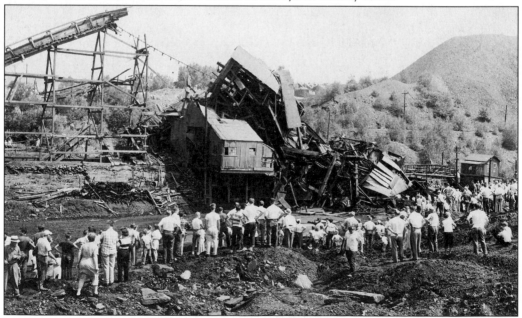

This Shenandoah breaker collapsed and killed and injured several men. Small breakers such as this were prone to collapse from the weight of the coal that they processed.

What may well have been one of the worst highway accidents in the history of the county occurred at the Red Church near Orwigsburg on June 2, 1959, when a propane tanker exploded, killing ten people and injuring twelve more. The terrific force of the explosion is shown by the damaged stone wall in front of the church.

Postal workers had to work hard to find, collect, and attempt to sort the mail that was being carried by this mail train when it collided with a truck near Port Carbon in 1949.

Aunt Nellie's Fine Foods are not in such fine shape after this accident occurred in front of the Reading Anthracite office building on Mahantongo Street in Pottsville in 1974.

When the East Penn Traction and Power Company trolley car barn in Palo Alto caught fire on January 6, 1917, it cut off power to all the trolley lines. Shoppers were stranded in Pottsville and were unable to go home until power was restored. This is what remained of the barn after the fire.

A fire that started in the Woolworth store on South Centre Street in Pottsville on December 17, 1914, destroyed the entire block. The only building that survived the fire was the Union Bank, which still stands today. The money that was in the vault of the Pennsylvania National Bank was not burned.

The Lyric Theater in New Philadelphia was destroyed by this fire in 1950. Cary Grant and Ann Sheridan starred in the last movie seen in the theater, *I Was a Male War Bride*. This image was carried by the Associated Press and it appeared in newspapers all over the country.

Firemen are spraying water on the roof of the Strand movie theater as part of their efforts to save buildings in the Shenandoah business district during this fire.

The F.W. Woolworth store was gutted in a fire that occurred in 1950. Rarings Shoe Store also suffered extensive damage. The two buildings were rebuilt and the old Woolworth store is now the location of the Schuylkill Chamber of Commerce.

An overturned Liberty Oil Co. tanker, a crushed pick-up truck, a damaged house, and four damaged cars was the scorecard for an accident that was similar to the one that took place at the Red Church in 1959. The accident happened on June 14, 1977, at West Market and Eighth Streets in Pottsville.

The scene of this airplane accident is being checked out by an aviation safety investigator. The plane crashed after it hit a power line when trying to make an emergency landing on May 5, 1973.